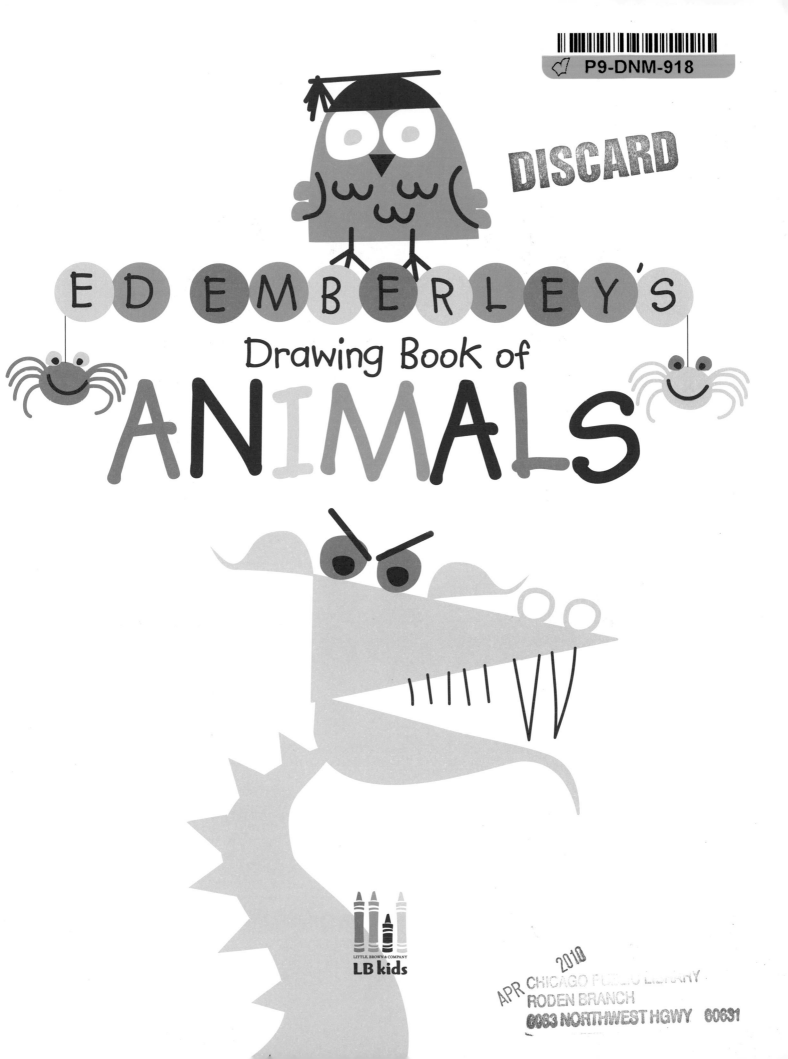

ED EMBERLEY'S
Drawing Book of
ANIMALS

P9-DNM-918

DISCARD

LITTLE, BROWN & COMPANY
LB kids

2010
APR CHICAGO PUBLIC LIBRARY
RODEN BRANCH
6083 NORTHWEST HGWY   60631

IF YOU CAN DRAW THESE SHAPES, LETTERS, NUMBERS AND THINGS —

YOU WILL BE ABLE TO DRAW ALL THE ANIMALS IN THIS BOOK.

FOR INSTANCE:

IN ORDER TO DRAW THIS POLLYWOG ⌒⌒● YOU USE THESE ● S · |

IN ORDER TO DRAW THIS BIRD 🐦 YOU USE THESE ⭕ D ▲▲ · ||| V V

THE DIAGRAMS ON THE FOLLOWING PAGES

WILL SHOW YOU HOW.

Happy drawing, Ed Emberley

SHAPES

Y J L
C D S
V W M
U

LETTERS

1 2 3

NUMBERS

.   SMALL DOT

•   LARGE DOT

↓   BIRD TRACK

     CURLICUE

WWWW   SCRATCHY SCRIBBLE

CURLY SCRIBBLE

THINGS

CHICAGO PUBLIC LIBRARY
RODEN BRANCH
6063 NORTHWEST HGWY 60631

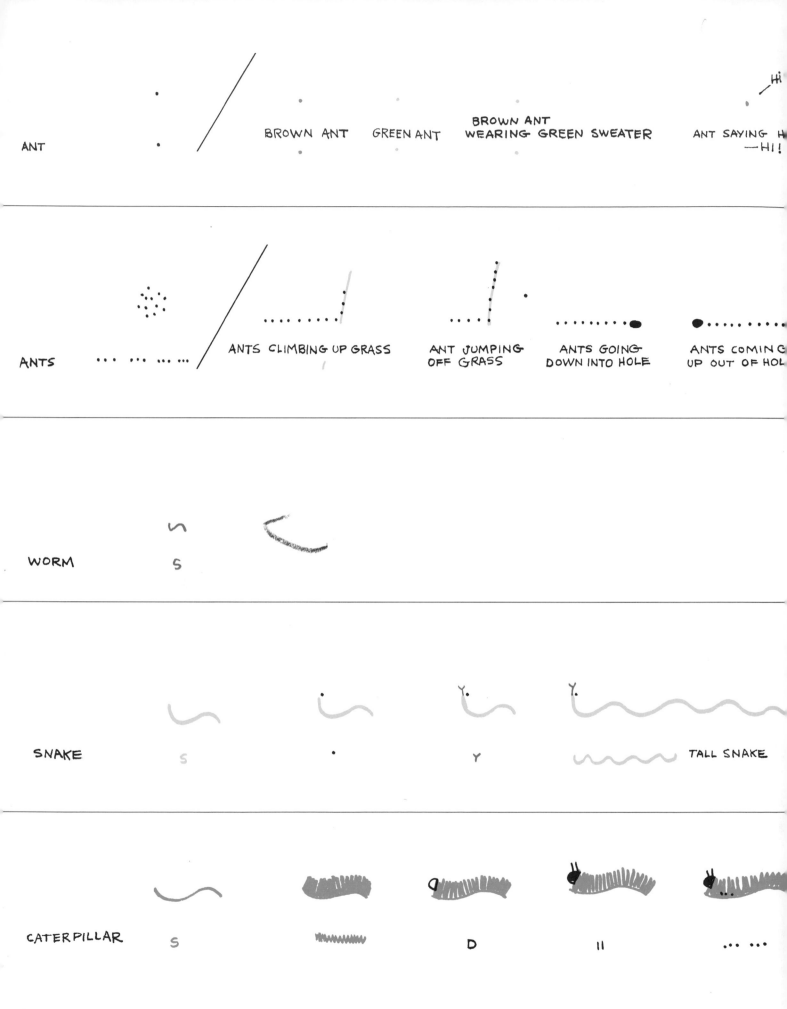

ANT

BROWN ANT GREEN ANT BROWN ANT WEARING GREEN SWEATER ANT SAYING HI —HI!

ANTS

ANTS CLIMBING UP GRASS ANT JUMPING OFF GRASS ANTS GOING DOWN INTO HOLE ANTS COMING UP OUT OF HOLE

WORM

SNAKE TALL SNAKE

CATERPILLAR

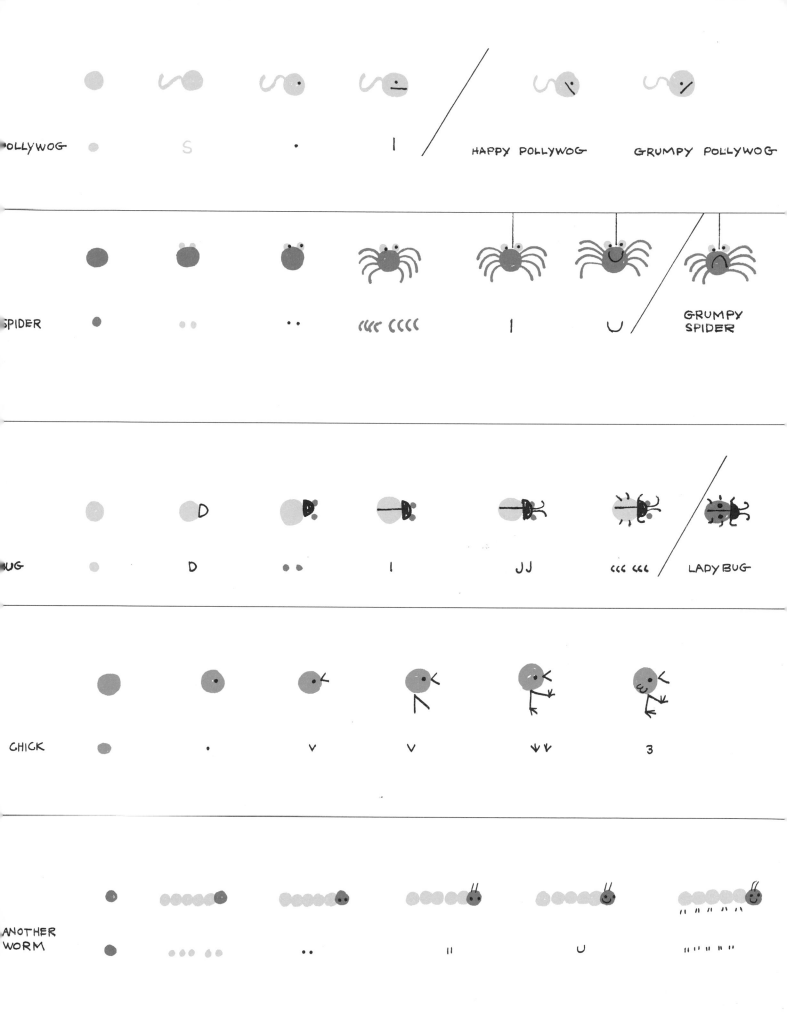

POLLYWOG   S   .   l   HAPPY POLLYWOG   GRUMPY POLLYWOG

SPIDER   .   ..   ..   ((((((l   U   GRUMPY SPIDER

BUG   D   ..   l   JJ   ((((((LADYBUG

CHICK   •   V   V   V V   3

ANOTHER WORM   ll   U   " " " " " "

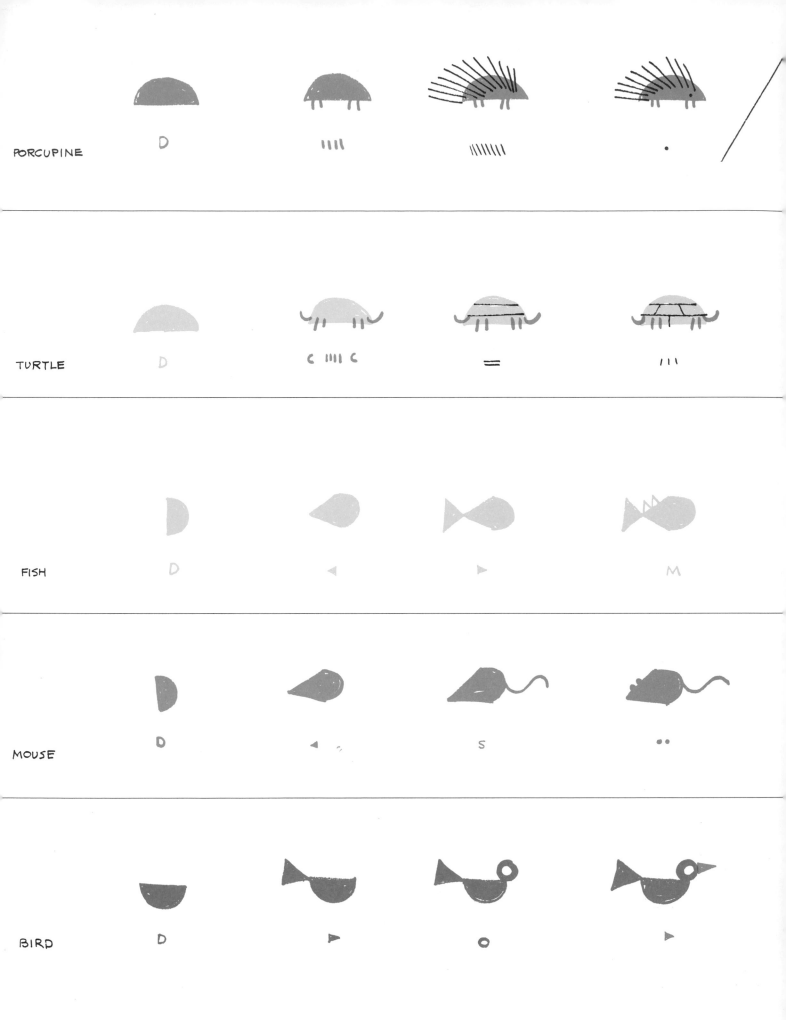

PORCUPINE

TURTLE

FISH

MOUSE

BIRD

6

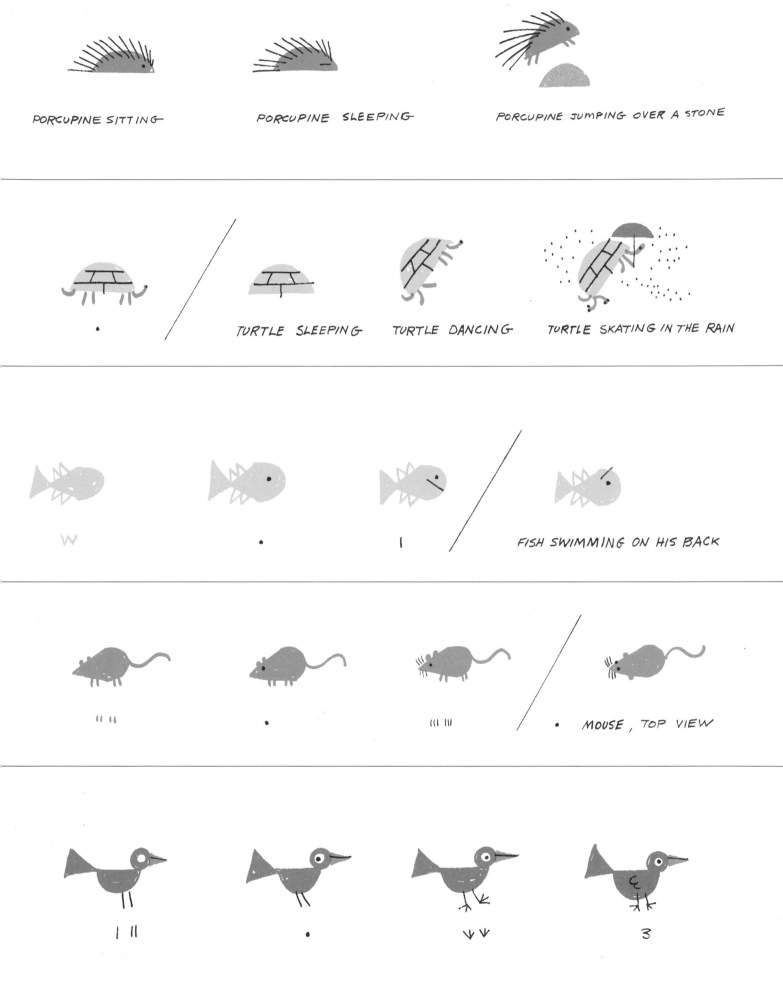

PORCUPINE SITTING

PORCUPINE SLEEPING

PORCUPINE JUMPING OVER A STONE

TURTLE SLEEPING

TURTLE DANCING

TURTLE SKATING IN THE RAIN

W

.

I

FISH SWIMMING ON HIS BACK

II II

.

III III

MOUSE, TOP VIEW

I II

.

V V

3

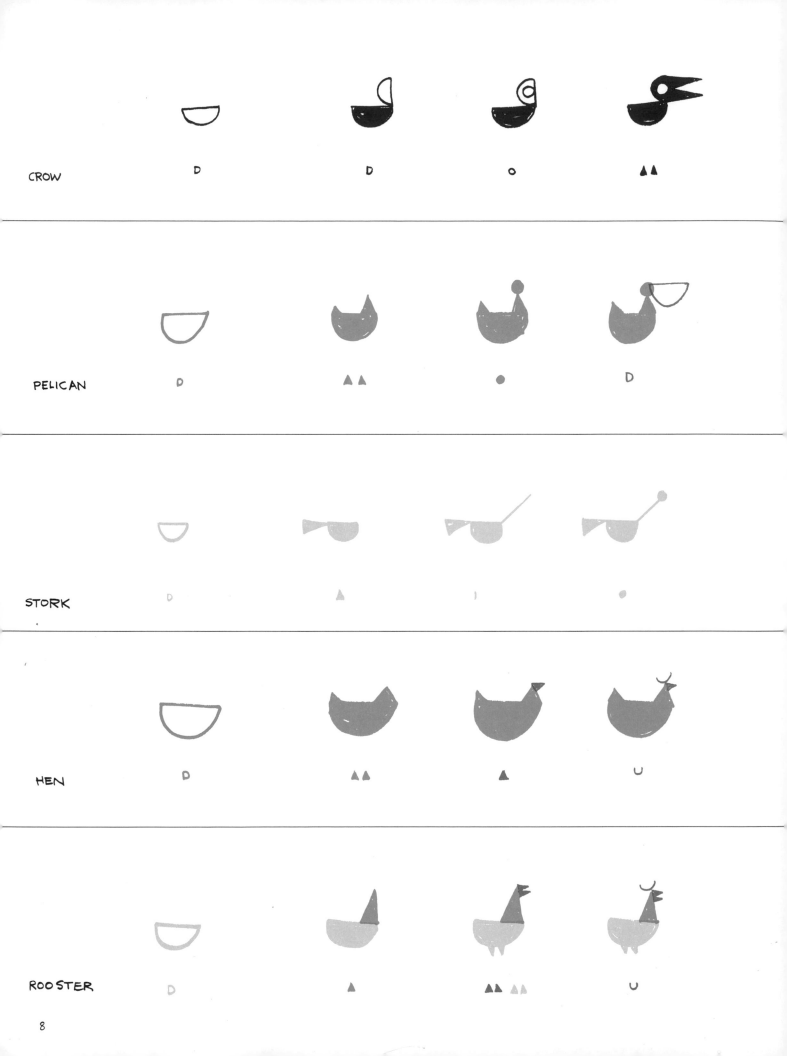

CROW

PELICAN

STORK

HEN

ROOSTER

8

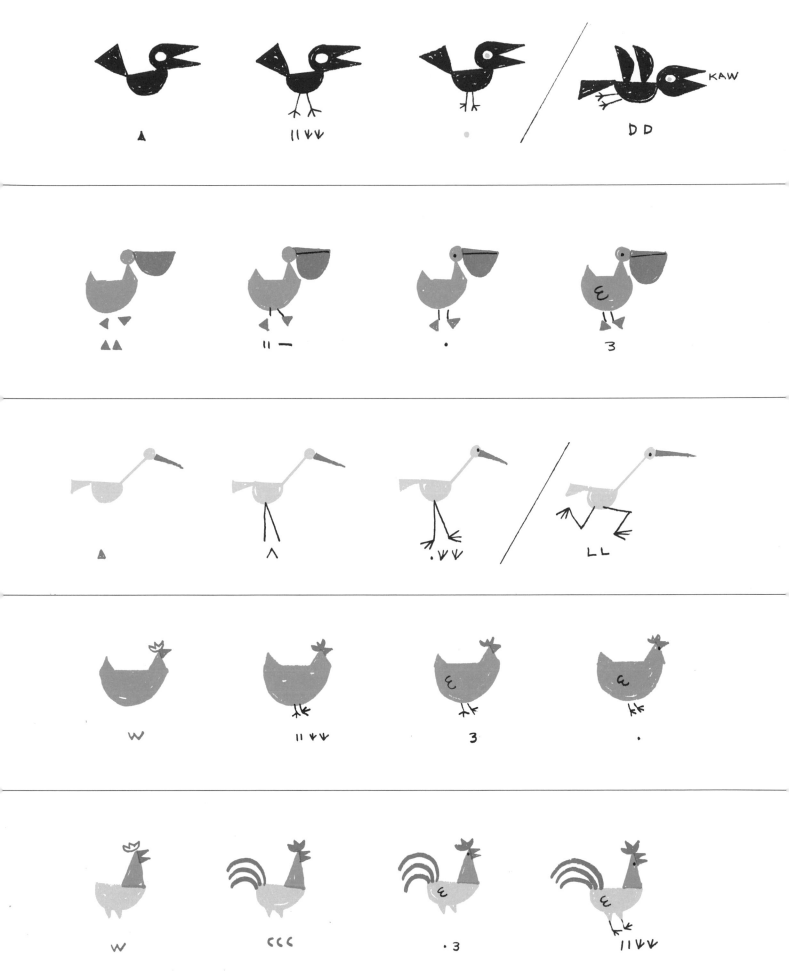

KAW

9

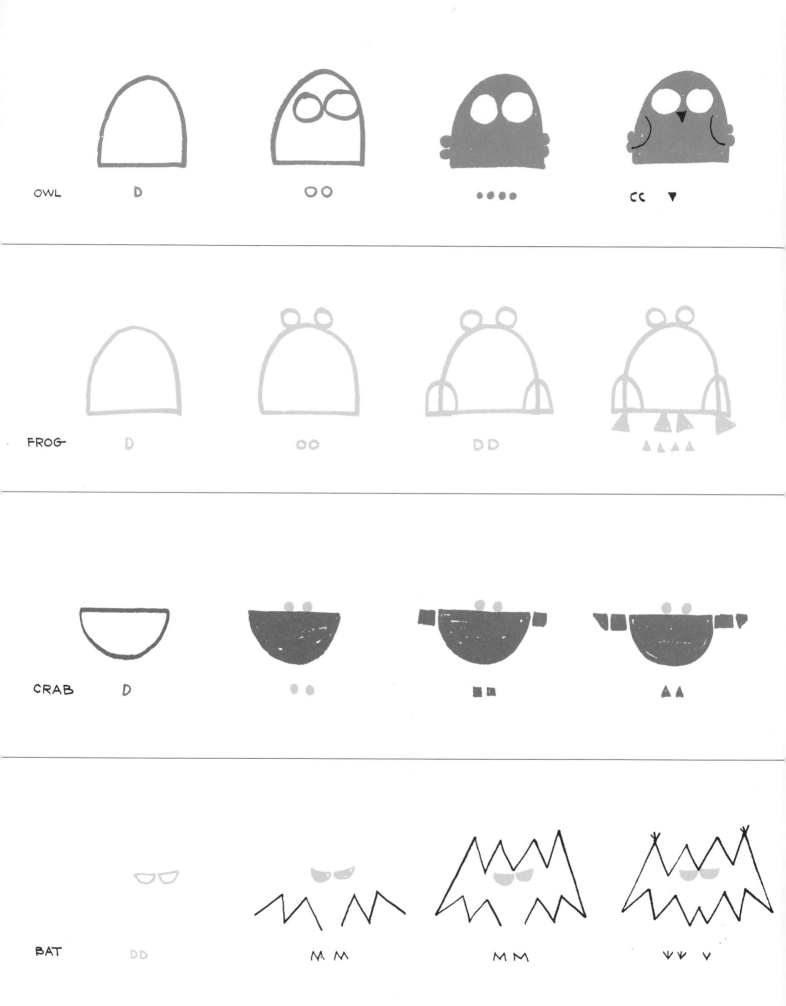

OWL   D   O O   ••••   C C   ▼

FROG   D   O O   D D   ▲▲▲▲

CRAB   D   • •   ▪ ▪   ▲ ▲

BAT   D D   M M   M M   V V   V

10

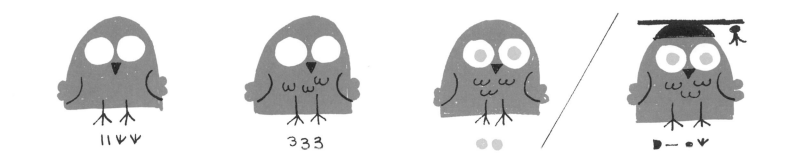

II↓↓   333   ••   D—●↓

II U   •• ●●   CROAKING FROG   SLEEPING FROG

DD   ▲▲   (((( ))))   JJ

•• I

BAT, BACK VIEW   BABY BAT

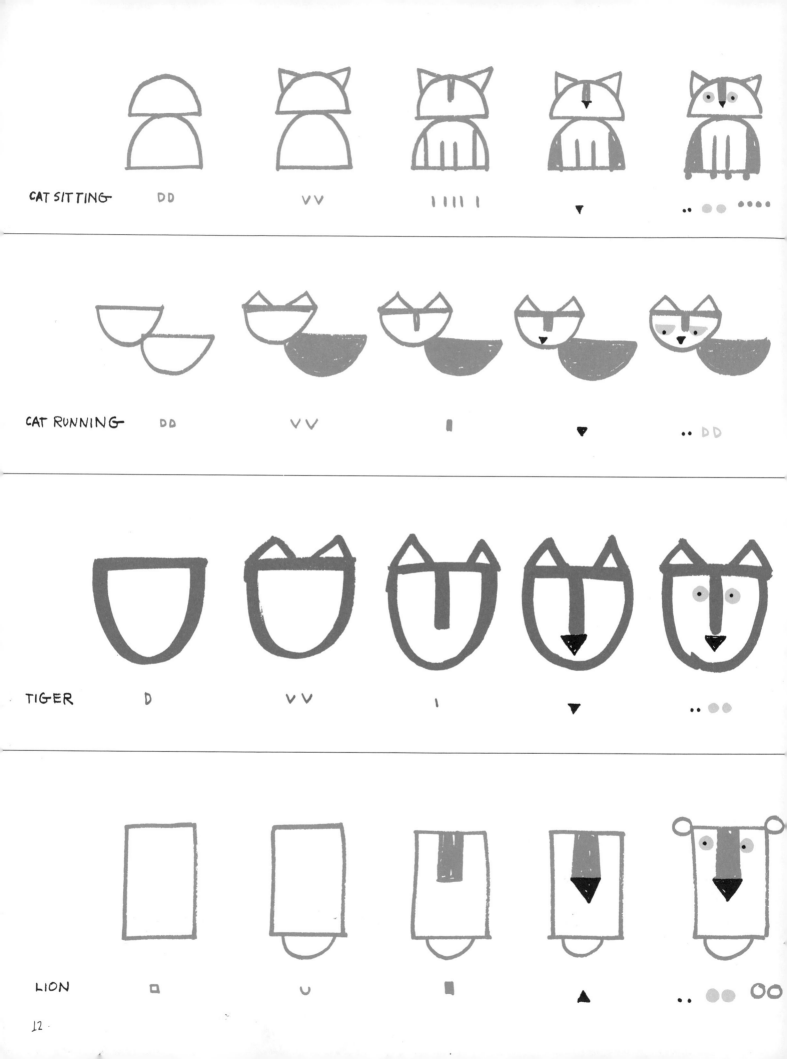

CAT SITTING   DD   V V   I I I I I   ▼   .. ●● ●●●●

CAT RUNNING   DD   V V   I   ▼   .. DD

TIGER   D   V V   I   ▼   .. ●●

LION   ▫   U   ▮   ▲   .. ●● OO

∪∪ J ∺ ∺ FAT CAT

J CCCC ,,,, ,, ,, ,,, | ((((((BLACK CAT RUNNING THE OTHER WAY

Y /// /// // ▲▲▲▲▲▲▲▲▲▲▲

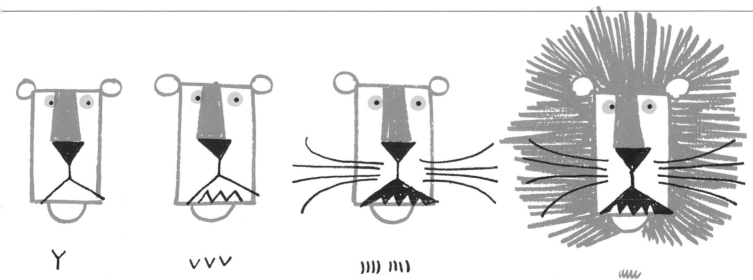

Y ∨∨∨))))))) ⋃⋃⋃⋃

13

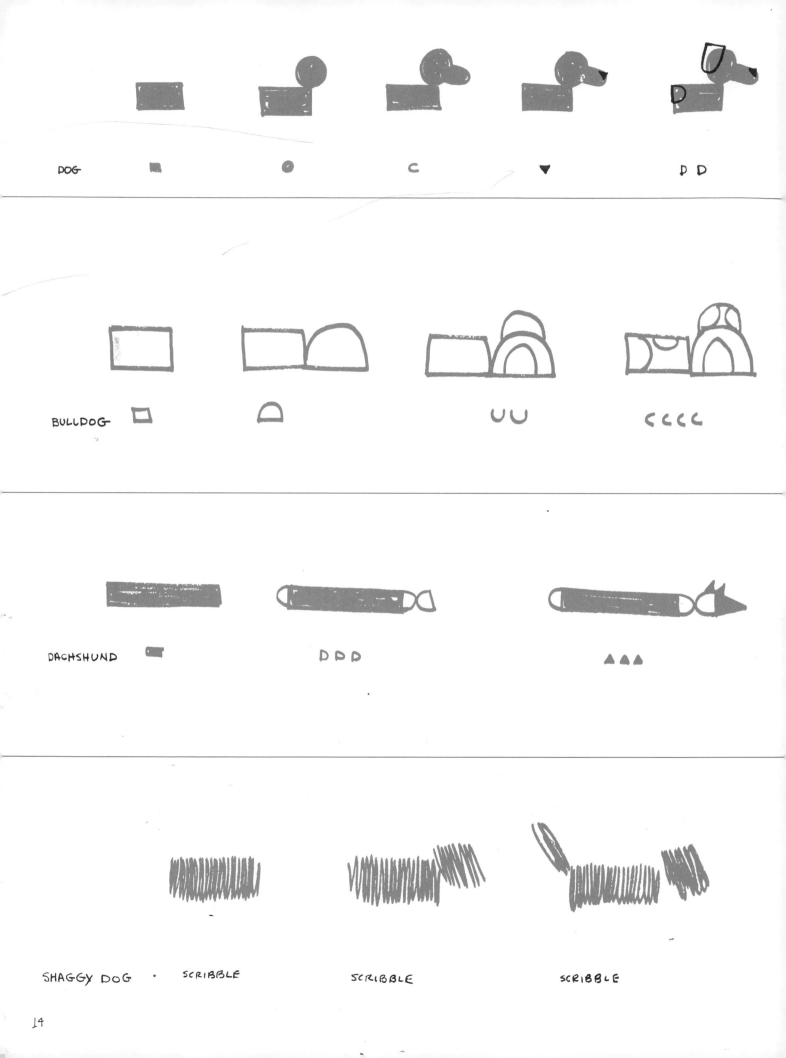

DOG

BULLDOG

DACHSHUND

SHAGGY DOG   •   SCRIBBLE   SCRIBBLE   SCRIBBLE

•●•••• |||| | | ᴵᴵ   DOG SITTING   DOG BEGGING

ᴸᴸ ᴸᴸ ᴸᴸ ᴸ   ●• •• ▼ ∧∧   = =   3 3

|| ||| ••   WEARING SWEATER

SCRIBBLE   ▲   ••Y

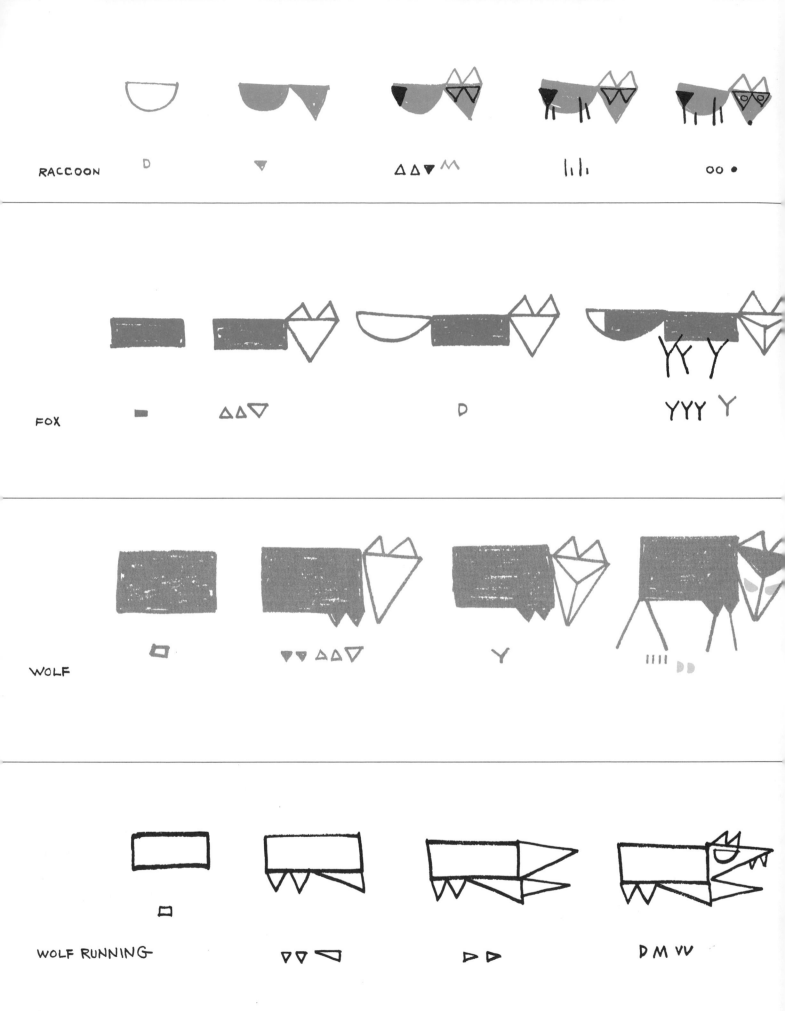

RACCOON

FOX

WOLF

WOLF RUNNING

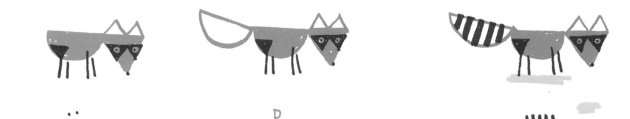

..   D   ııııı

.. C   / ‹‹‹ ‹‹‹   •••• •• •

... S   S ııı ııı ııı ııı ııı   WOLF LOOKING THE OTHER WAY

▲ ● ııııı •   S ‹‹‹ ıııı •

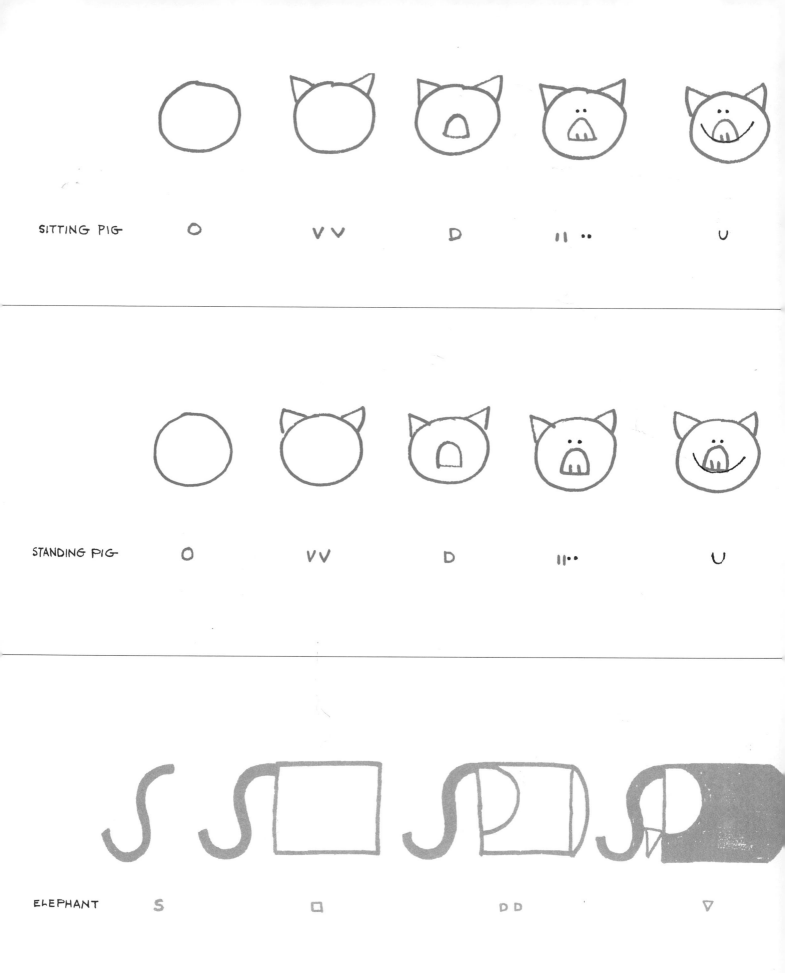

SITTING PIG O   V V   D || ··   U

STANDING PIG O   V V   D || ··   U

ELEPHANT   S   □   D D   ▽

CC   1   22   @ VV

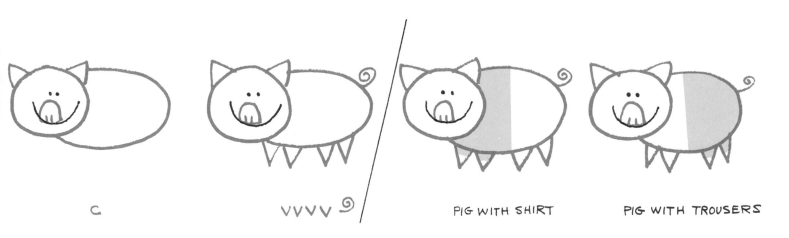

C   VVVV @   PIG WITH SHIRT   PIG WITH TROUSERS

■■■■ C   ᴜ ᴜ ᴜ ᴜ ᴜ ᴜ ᴜ ᴜ •   CV   • ELEPHANT LOOKING AT YOU

HORSE

DEER

GOAT

SHEEP

I SSSSS

DONKEY

UNICORN

ΔDD

U

YYYY

DEER EATING

GOATS BUTTING

D • •

I W

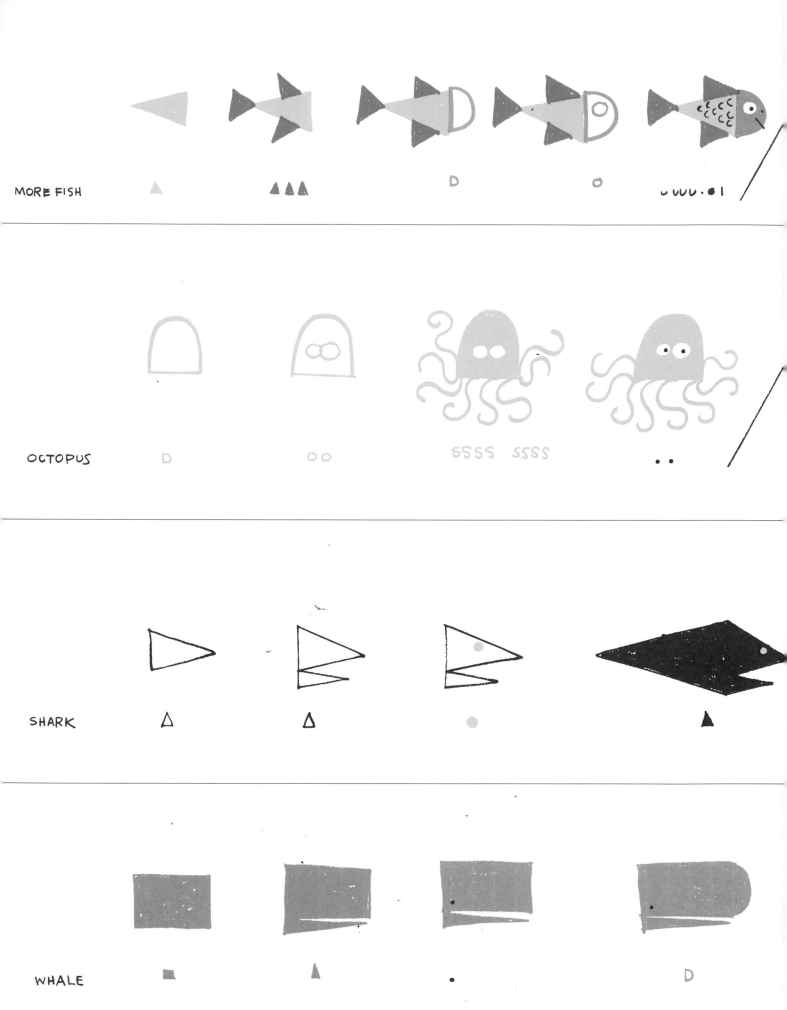

MORE FISH

OCTOPUS

SHARK

WHALE

OCTOPUS LOOKING UP   SMILING OCTOPUS   MEAN OCTOPUS

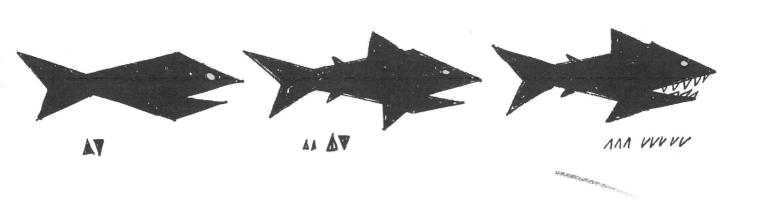

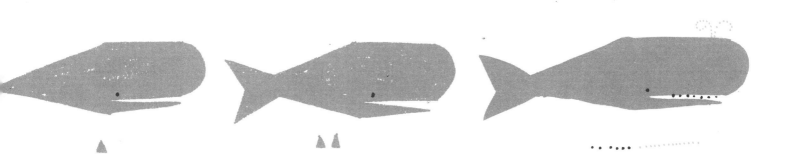

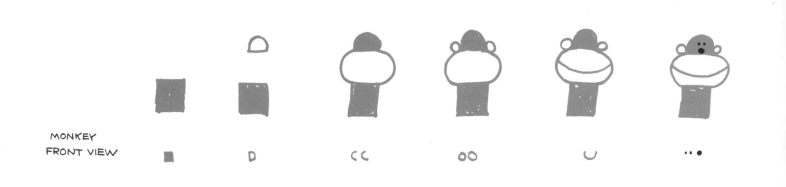

MONKEY FRONT VIEW

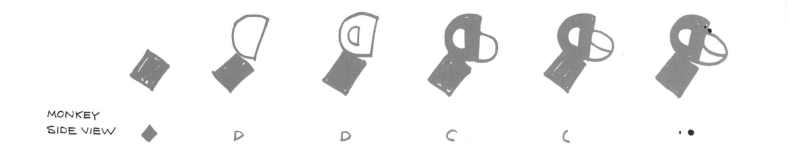

MONKEY SIDE VIEW

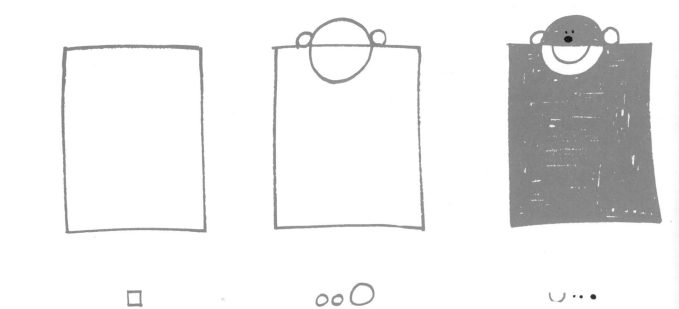

GORILLA

CCCC

• • • ▪ ▪ ▪ ○

CCCC ℰ

oo oo – —

▼ ▼ ▪

LLLL

• • • • • • • ∨ CCCCC CCCCC CCCCC CCCCC

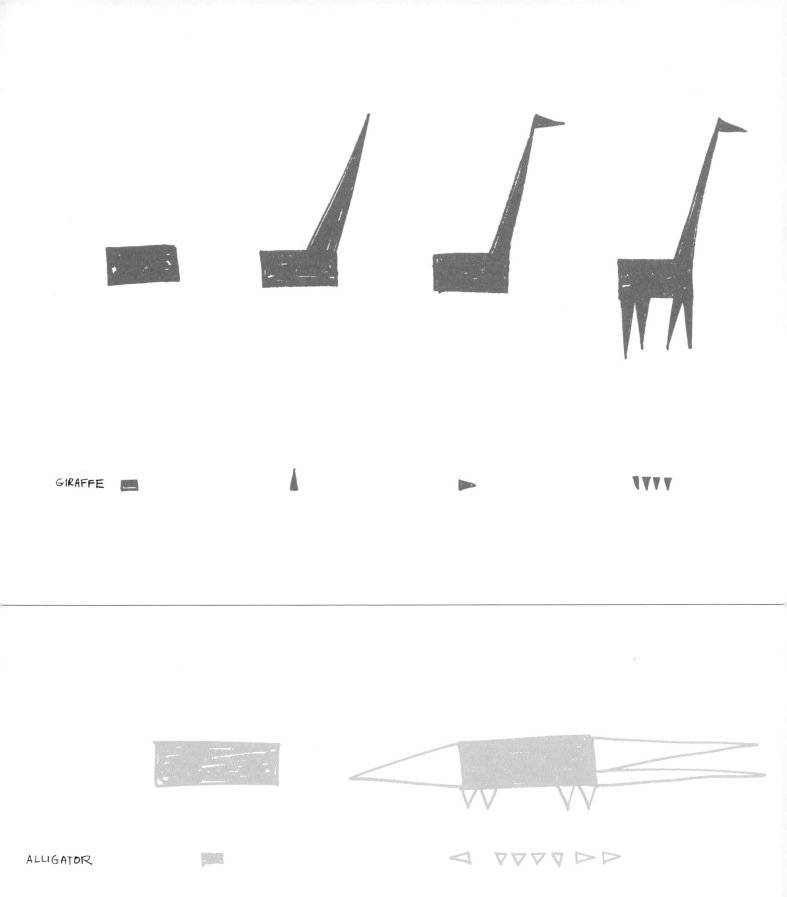

GIRAFFE

ALLIGATOR

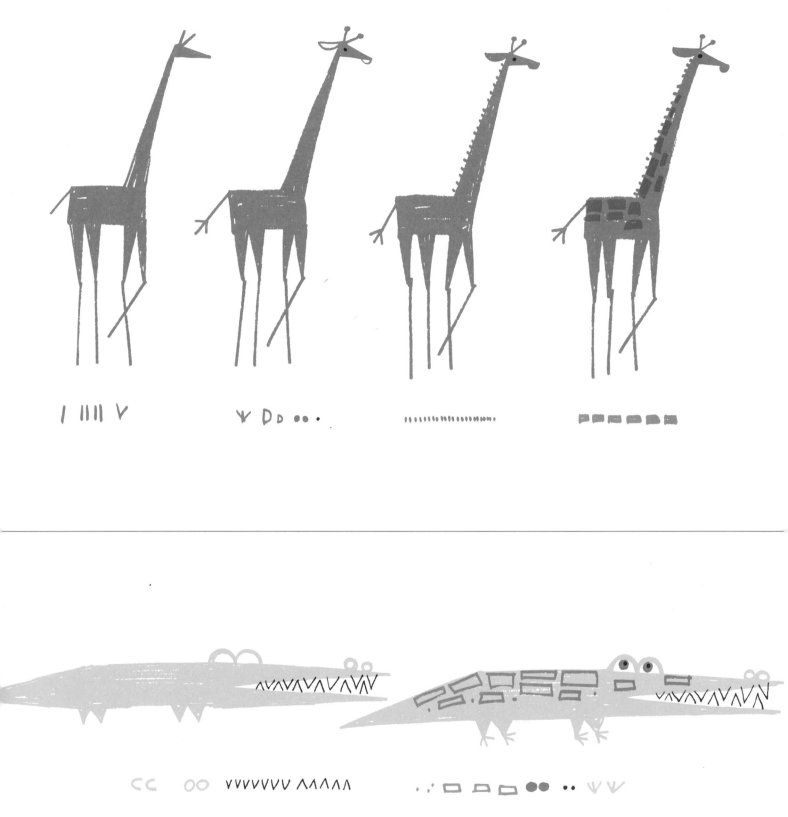

DRAGON   D

SSS

SS

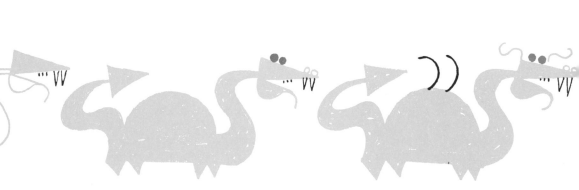

▲▲ VV VV I   VV‚‚‚

●● ∘∘

SS   CC

/ /I II II   MM V

▲▲ ▲▲▲▲▲▲▲▲▲

..

THERE ARE MANY WAYS YOU CAN
CHANGE THE BASIC DRAWINGS.
YOU CAN...

CHANGE
COLOR

CHANGE
SIZE

MAKE ONE
PART LARGER

MAKE ONE
PART SMALLER

DECORATE

DECORATE

PECKING

LOOKING UP

LOOKING BACK

SITTING

SINGING

RUNNING

AND SUGGESTIONS

YOU CAN MAKE PEOPLE AND ANIMALS
LOOK SAD, HAPPY, MEAN, EMBARRASSED OR
GRUMPY BY CHANGING THEIR
EYEBROWS AND/OR MOUTHS, LIKE THIS...

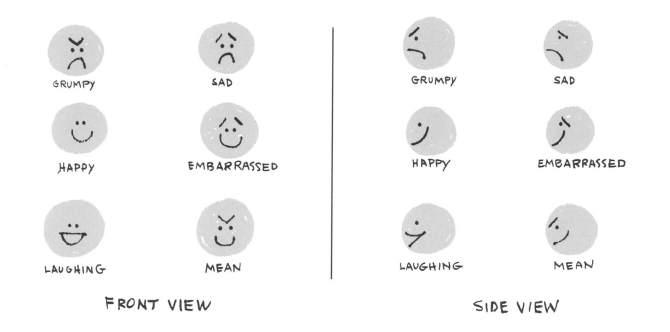

GRUMPY   SAD

HAPPY   EMBARRASSED

LAUGHING   MEAN

FRONT VIEW

GRUMPY   SAD

HAPPY   EMBARRASSED

LAUGHING   MEAN

SIDE VIEW

YOU CAN USE THIS SIMPLE METHOD OF
DRAWING TO BLOCK IN MORE COMPLICATED
DRAWINGS. FOR INSTANCE...

BLOCK IN   FILL IN   EMBELLISH

FOR THE BOY I WAS,
THE BOOK I COULD NOT FIND

Copyright © 1970 by Edward R. Emberley

Cover and title page illustrations copyright © 2006 by Edward R. Emberley

All rights reserved. Except as permitted under
the U.S. Copyright Act of 1976, no part of this publication
may be reproduced, distributed, or transmitted in any form
or by any means, or stored in a database or retrieval system,
without the prior written permission of the publisher.

Little, Brown Books for Young Readers

Hachette Book Group

237 Park Avenue, New York, NY, 10017

Visit our Web site at www.lb-kids.com

LB kids is an imprint of Little, Brown Books for Young Readers. The LB kids
name and logo are trademarks of Hachette Book Group, Inc.

First Revised Paperback Edition: April 2006

First Paperback Edition: September 1994

Originally published in hardcover in April 1970 by Little, Brown and Company

10 9 8 7 6 5 4

ISBN 978-0-316-78979-0

WKT

Printed in China